PIKU'S PICKLES

A Guide to Starting Up Your Own Gig as a Child

Krish Gupta

ISBN 979-8-89026-726-9

A PLAN
TO PICKLE
Krish Gupta

Our memories are rooted in scents, sounds, and colours, often resurfacing as nostalgia as seasons change, or suddenly evoked by the aroma of a childhood dish or perhaps the sight of a long-forgotten, favourite item. That afternoon, Piku's walk to his grandmother's home was punctuated by frequent halts as he inhaled the sweet fragrance of blooming flowers and raw mangoes that dangled above. This was a surprisingly green neighbourhood, dotted with mango trees that poked their heads out like curious children, their green fruits appearing ripe for the picking.

As Piku gazed at the afternoon sky, he could almost taste the spicy aromas of his grandmother's pickles, and his mouth watered in anticipation. The summer season transported him back to the soothing familiarity of her cooking, and it felt like a warm hug. As the years passed by, the pickles had become an enduring reminder of happy memories from his childhood.

"Please, just one more spoonful, Dadi," Piku pleaded.

"Piku beta, you might get a stomach ache if you eat any more pickle!" cautioned his grandmother.

"I know, Dadi, but it's just too delicious to resist, especially with these hot, fresh aloo paranthas," Piku replied.

Seated at the dining table, Piku gazed out of the window, watching as the golden rays of the afternoon sun slowly faded into the deep blue hues of evening. Yet, the mouthwatering aroma wafting from his plate commanded equal attention. More than the fluffy parathas, it was the pickle that he savored with unabashed relish, nibbling on it as if it were a batch of freshly-baked cookies.

It was so delicious, he simply couldn't put it down!

Rekha's heart swelled with affection and contentment as she watched her grandson devour her pickles with unbridled gusto. The sight reminded her of her own childhood, and the cherished recipes her mother had passed down to her. In a world that had changed so dramatically since her youth, with its bustling metropolises and ever-changing landscapes, the familiar taste of her mother's pickle served as a poignant reminder of simpler, happier times.

As her mind wandered back to memories of carefree mango-picking afternoons and endless outdoor picnics, a sudden crash from the kitchen shattered her peaceful contemplation.

"Oh no, Dadi, I'm so sorry!" cried Piku, his eyes brimming with tears as he surveyed the shattered mason jar and the delectable mango pickle that lay in ruins on the kitchen floor, intermingled with shards of glass.

As the duo surveyed the red-tinged mess that lined the floor, the unmistakable aroma of Rekha's pickles filled the air. The pungent scent evoked memories of Rekha's childhood, of days spent in the company of her mother, learning the secrets of the perfect pickle recipes. The warmth of those memories mixed with the tangy, savoury aroma, and Rekha couldn't help but shed a tear as she surveyed the broken jar and its contents.

The broken jar, with a deep crack running through its center, served as a poignant metaphor for Rekha's own struggles and unfulfilled ambitions. As a young girl, she had dreamed of becoming a successful businessperson, financially independent and able to stand on her own feet. Yet, the reality of her life had turned out very differently, filled with unexpected obstacles and setbacks that had forced her to put her dreams on hold.

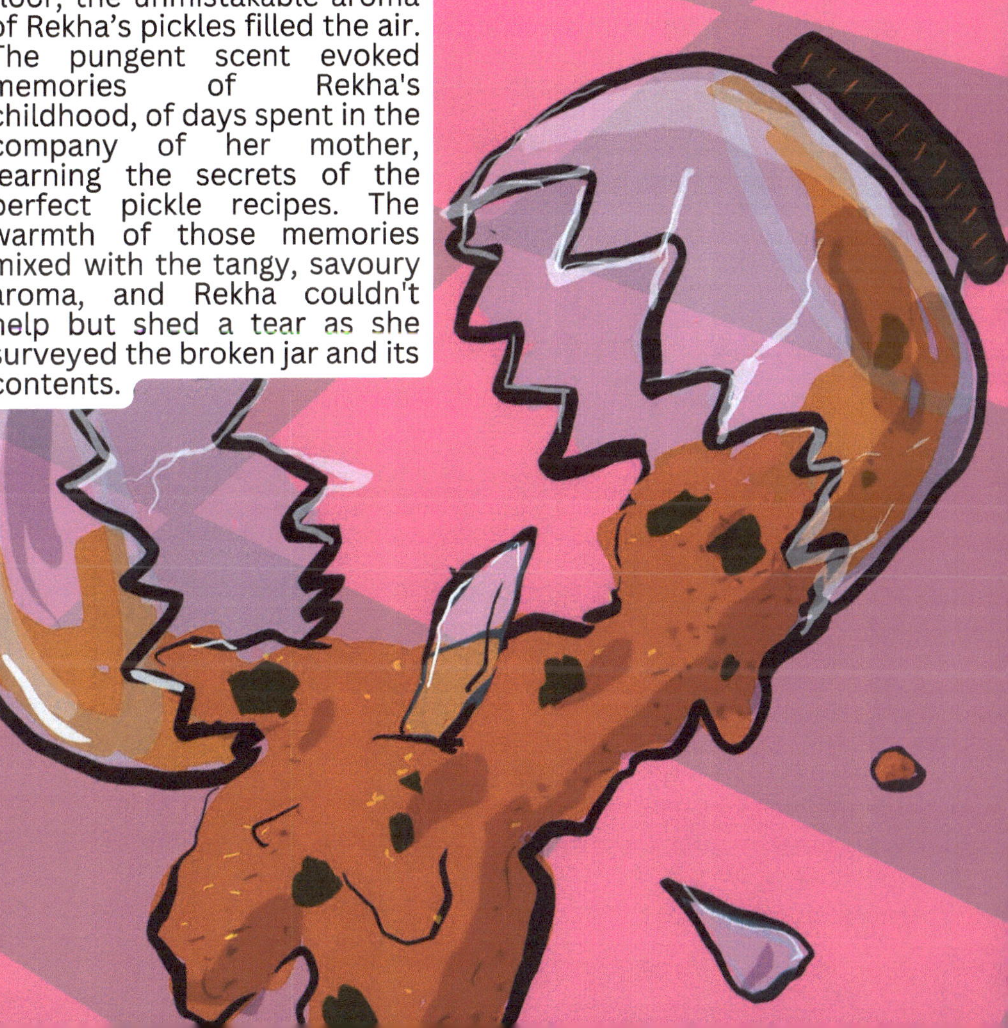

"Dadi, is everything alright?" asked Piku, his voice soft and gentle. He wiped the tears that streamed down his own cheeks.
Rekha dried her eyes and assured Piku, "Don't worry, I'm fine." However, she now acknowledged that her current state was a significant part of the problem, that throughout her life she had never felt that she was thriving. Her numerous aspirations and dreams had been left unfulfilled as she focused on taking care of her family and managing the household. "So many possibilities, so many desires, all left unexplored..." she trailed off, lost in thought.
Piku had never seen this side of his grandmother before, and he was taken aback. Rekha had always seemed content with her life, happy to dote on her grandchildren and bask in her family's adoration. However, he had learned something new today, and he resolved to help his Dadi in any way he could. He squeezed her hand tightly as they both stood over the kitchen counter, looking down at the spilled pickle.

Rekha feverishly tried to gather the shards of the broken pickle jar, attempting to mend it. In an instant, a spark of inspiration ignited within her, and she let go of the glass pieces to grasp her grandson's shoulders with elation. "Piku, I have found the glue that will help me piece my life back together!" she exclaimed.
Piku was taken aback by his grandmother's sudden change in demeanour and struggled to comprehend what was happening in their cosy kitchen. Sensing his confusion, Rekha clarified, "I want to start my own business."
Piku's eyes widened in astonishment, unable to believe what he had just heard from his grandmother.

As Rekha frantically paced around the kitchen, she exclaimed, "My pickles have been the talk of the town for years! I serve them to anyone who comes over, whether it's for breakfast, lunch, or dinner. And everyone always enjoys them, no matter what flavour they are. Why didn't I act on this earlier?"
Piku could sense the frustration in his grandmother's voice and felt deep empathy for her. Rekha had hinted at this business idea before, but her family always dismissed it as a joke. This time, Piku was determined to help her realise her dream.
"Dadi, you're right. This is a brilliant idea, and we should definitely pursue it. But we need to develop a business plan and start working on it immediately," he said with enthusiasm.
As Rekha leaned forward and planted a kiss on his forehead, she felt more inspired than ever before.

Piku rummaged through his old supplies and brought out a whiteboard and markers. He set it up in the living room, ready to dive into their business plan. The duo began brainstorming ideas, bouncing thoughts off each other with contagious enthusiasm. Their creativity filled the room, and the possibilities seemed endless.

"The first step to starting a business is to think about what products we can sell," said Piku, putting on his thinking cap.

Rekha thought for a moment and replied, "Let's start with three flavours of pickles -- mango, lime, and mixed vegetables. These three are relatively easier to prepare, go well with almost anything, and also have a longer shelf life," suggested Rekha.

"That's a great idea, Dadi! Those are important factors to consider," encouraged Piku.

"Now, let's research the various kinds of pickles that are currently being sold in the market, and where we stand in comparison."

As they browsed through an online store, they realised that they weren't the only ones with a home business idea. How could they differentiate themselves?

Dadi's Pickle Plan

Flavours to make:

1. Mango
2. Lime
3. Mixed vegetable

Name Ideas
Rekha's Pickles
Natural Taste Pickles
Lovely Home Pickles

Homemade pickles, made with natural ingredients using family recipes

"Ah, Piku, I have an idea to set us apart from the rest," said Rekha, a glimmer of entrepreneurial brilliance in her eye. "While other products are all mass-produced in factories, my pickles are made from a traditional recipe that has been handed down through three generations of women. Each batch is carefully crafted by hand in my kitchen, infusing every jar with the essence of pristine India. It's something that customers of all ages can appreciate."

Impressed, Piku replied, "You're absolutely right, Dadi. Additionally, the current market prices for pickles are quite steep, especially considering the small quantities that are offered. However, we could launch our product at a more accessible price point and then gradually raise it as our customer base expands. This way, we can evaluate our profit and loss model accordingly."

Rekha beamed with pride, watching her grandson display a mature understanding of business strategy. She marvelled at how quickly he was growing up.

By diligently researching and strategizing, Piku and Rekha developed their business strategy. They turned to various websites and e-books on business management, grateful for the abundance of resources available online. The vast array of information and success stories served as a valuable source of inspiration and guidance for the two entrepreneurs.

Through three days of tireless planning and brainstorming, Piku became increasingly invested in their business plan. He was so absorbed in the process that he felt reluctant to return to school the following day. However, while packing his bag, he suddenly remembered an important detail and dashed to his grandmother.

“Dadi, we forgot something crucial!” he exclaimed. “We haven't come up with a name for our brand yet!”

Rekha's eyes sparkled with pride as she gave Piku a tight hug. “Our brand will be called 'Piku's Pickles',” she declared.

Krish Gupta

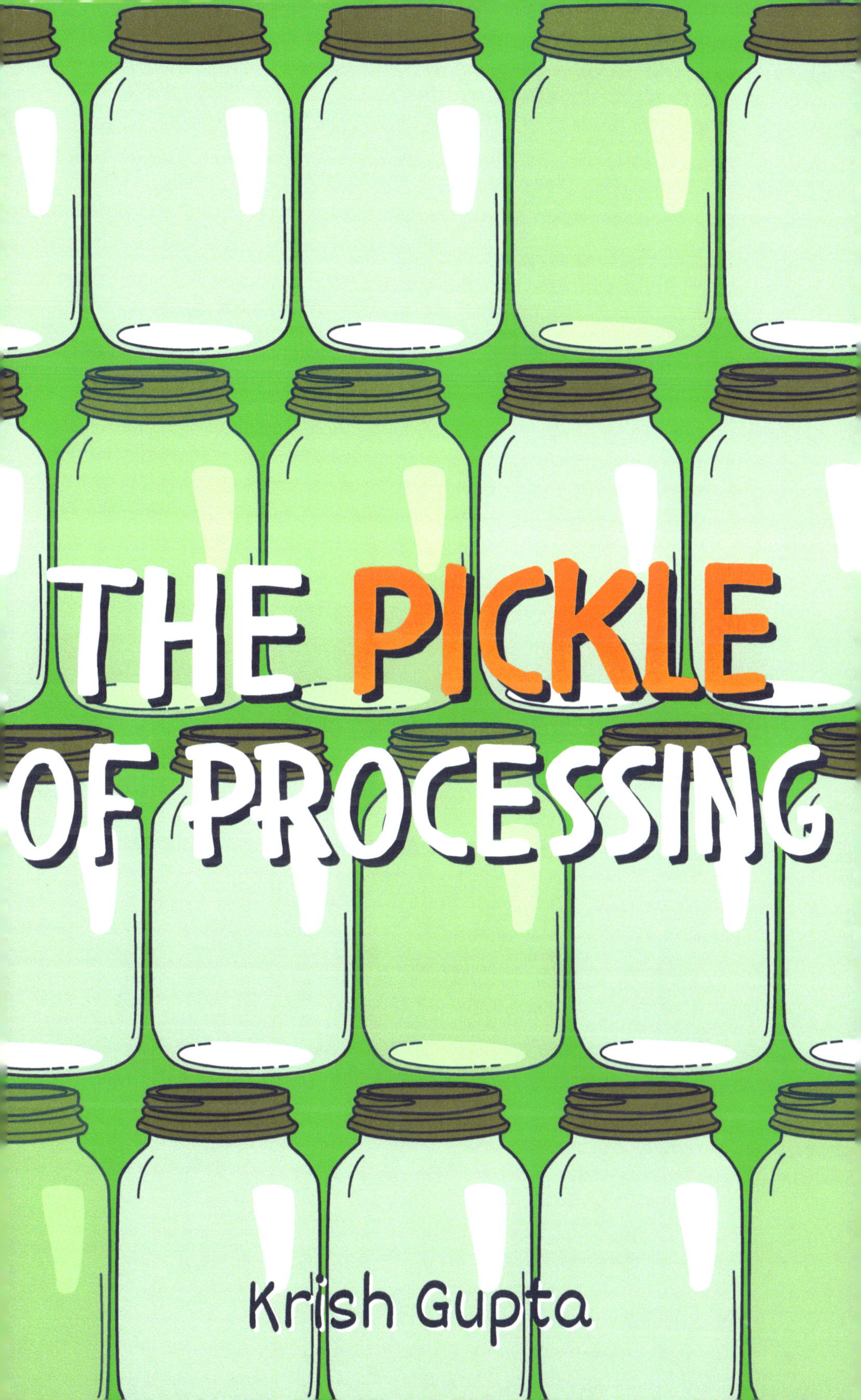
THE PICKLE
OF PROCESSING
Krish Gupta

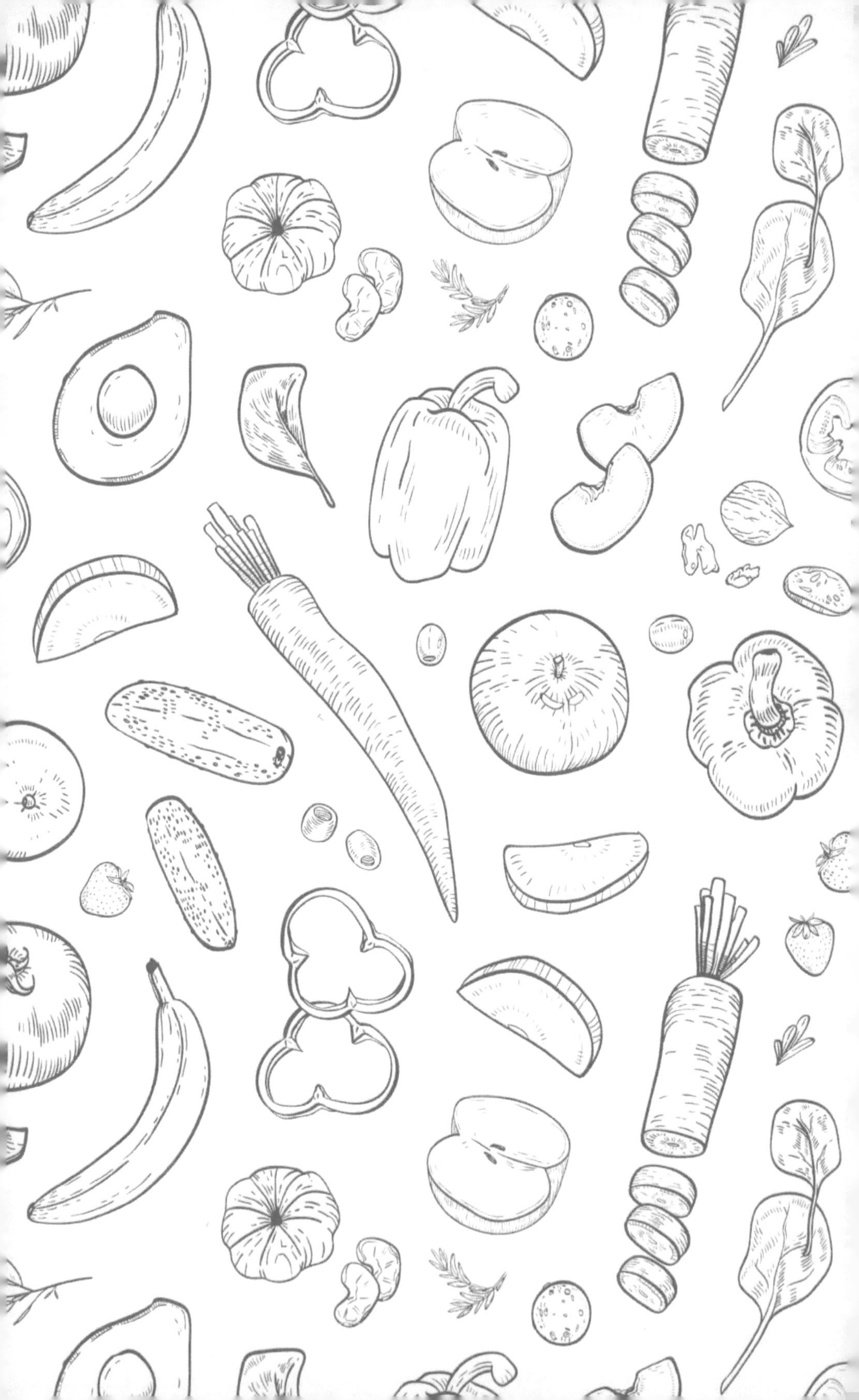

Two weeks had passed since Piku and Rekha had embarked on their journey to launch Piku's Pickles, their home business. They had made considerable progress with Piku's Pickles, spending hours each day browsing business websites and strategizing late into the night. Amidst the daily hustle-bustle, the two found moments of joy in their shared passion and commitment to turning their dream into a reality.

As a first step, they knew they needed an eye-catching logo that truly represented their brand. Rekha sought out her next-door neighbor, a lively graphic designer who had enjoyed her delicious pickles on multiple occasions. With his help, together, they created a bright red and yellow logo, featuring the words "Piku's Pickles" in a striking font. “This logo will surely attract buyers!” exclaimed Piku, elated at the outcome.

• PIKU'S •

PICKLES

Natural • Homemade • Traditional

As Rekha and Piku contemplated the next step in their business plan, they realized they needed to determine their target audience. Rekha shared, with a hint of jest, "I'm sure everyone will love my pickles!" Piku, on the other hand, knew they needed to be precise about identifying the customers who would be interested in buying their product. “Of course they will, Dadi!” encouraged Piku. “But we need to find out exactly which customers will be willing and able to purchase the pickles. That will help us settle on a target group of people which will inform our marketing strategies as well!” To achieve this, the two collaborated to brainstorm and generate a list of potential customer bases.

They ultimately decided to market to individuals aged 30-50, who were known to consume pickles regularly with their meals: a group that represented a significant proportion of pickle consumers in the market.

Now that they knew who they wanted to sell their pickles to, they felt very excited about their business. They were proud of all the work they had done so far and couldn't wait to see their brand come to life.

One afternoon, Rekha was picking Piku up from school when they found themselves in the midst of a disagreement. Rekha's friend, who owned a home-based bakery, had suggested that Rekha should start marketing their brand. Acting upon her friend's advice, Rekha had begun promoting their pickles.
However, Piku pointed out that the manufacturing, production, and packaging of the pickles had not yet been finalized, and it was too early to think about marketing their product.
“Dadi, I appreciate your friend's advice, but we can’t rush into marketing so soon! As someone who is fairly active on social media, I'm concerned that we may not gain enough followers if we launch on social media prematurely. It's critical to ensure all aspects of our strategy are well planned and executed, or our entire strategy might fail,” Piku exclaimed.

Rekha was taken aback at Piku's sudden outburst, but she knew that it stemmed from his passion and enthusiasm. She was only just realizing the complex technological factors involved, and was becoming increasingly anxious about launching the pickle business. Could she really do this all on her own? Even though Piku and some of her friends were proving to be incredibly helpful, feelings of self-doubt were beginning to take over.

Sensing his grandmother's distress, Piku stopped walking to give her a tight hug. "Dadi, don't stress. We've got this! With our combined efforts, this business will be a roaring success, and Rekha's pickles will be the talk of the town!"

Rekha corrected him with a smile as she hugged him back. "Actually it's Piku's Pickles. I may not be as tech-savvy as you, beta, and I hadn't considered all the other processes involved, but I trust you. Your belief in this venture is more than enough for me!"

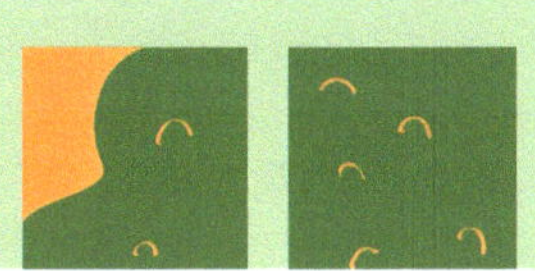

Piku and Rekha put their heads together to brainstorm the next stage of their business - planning for packaging and production of the pickles.

They went to the local market and purchased several mason jars and the required raw materials for their pickles. They also printed several professional-looking stickers with their logo from a nearby printing shop. Upon returning home, they set up an efficient production line on Rekha's kitchen counters and admired the first few building blocks of Piku's Pickles.

Rekha got started on making the pickles, while Piku was her little helper, bustling around the kitchen and following her instructions to wash, peel, or pass any ingredients. The pair spent the next few hours filling the bottles to the brim with the tangy pickle mixture. After placing the last of the jars in the fridge, they gave each other a high-five and retired to bed, exhausted from the day's work.

After a few days had passed, Piku and Rekha decided to taste the pickles they had made. However, to their dismay, they noticed that the pickles had gone slightly stale and were giving off a rancid smell. "Oh dear, it's the preservatives," Rekha lamented. "We forgot to add them in to extend the shelf life of the pickles."

"Don't worry, Dadi," Piku comforted her. "We'll figure it out." After some research, Piku came across sodium benzoate, which was cited as the ideal preservative for pickles, and claimed to increase their shelf life by several months.

"Interesting," Rekha remarked. "I've always used conventional preservatives like salt and sugar, but I've never made pickles on such a large scale before. I thought the citric acid in the limes and mangoes would act as a natural preservative. Let's give sodium benzoate a try. We learn something new every day, don't we, Piku?" Rekha said with a good-natured chuckle.

With a newfound understanding of the use of preservatives in the pickling process, Piku and Rekha were determined to make sure that their next batch of pickles would be perfect.

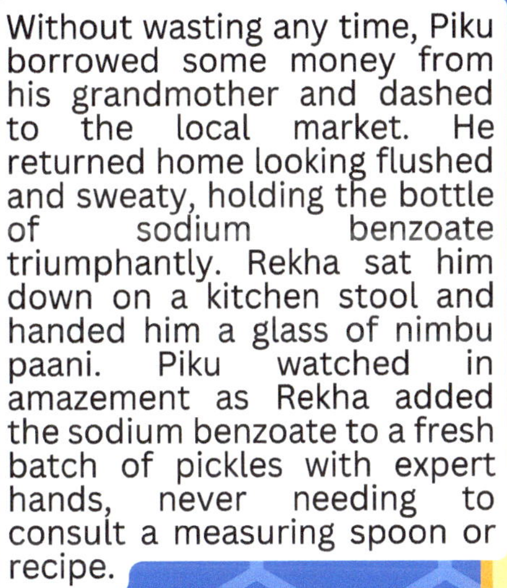

Without wasting any time, Piku borrowed some money from his grandmother and dashed to the local market. He returned home looking flushed and sweaty, holding the bottle of sodium benzoate triumphantly. Rekha sat him down on a kitchen stool and handed him a glass of nimbu paani. Piku watched in amazement as Rekha added the sodium benzoate to a fresh batch of pickles with expert hands, never needing to consult a measuring spoon or recipe.

Rekha offered Piku a taste. He licked his lips, savoring the enhanced flavors, pure bliss spreading across his face as he went in for seconds. "Piku! Put that down! We don't want to finish all the pickles now, do we?" Rekha chuckled, playfully swiping the bowl away from Piku's hands.

Piku, who couldn't resist the delectable taste of his grandmother's culinary masterpiece, couldn't wait for the rest of the world to savor her pickles.

With great care, Rekha stored the freshly made pickle jars in the fridge, letting the cool temperature work its preserving magic. The duo eagerly awaited the outcome of their efforts, giving the sodium benzoate a full month to infuse into the mixture. During this time, Rekha had to keep a close eye on Piku, who couldn't resist opening the refrigerator door several times a day, drooling in anticipation.
After a month had passed, the pair sat down to taste their creation, and were ecstatic with the zesty and tangy flavors of the pickles. "They've never tasted this amazing before!" Rekha exclaimed with joy, while Piku could only nod in agreement, too busy devouring the pickles to speak. With their product nearly ready to hit the market and wow customers, Rekha and Piku were thrilled to see their vision coming to fruition, and were filled with excitement for what the future held.
PIKU'S PICKLES
PIKU'S PICKLES

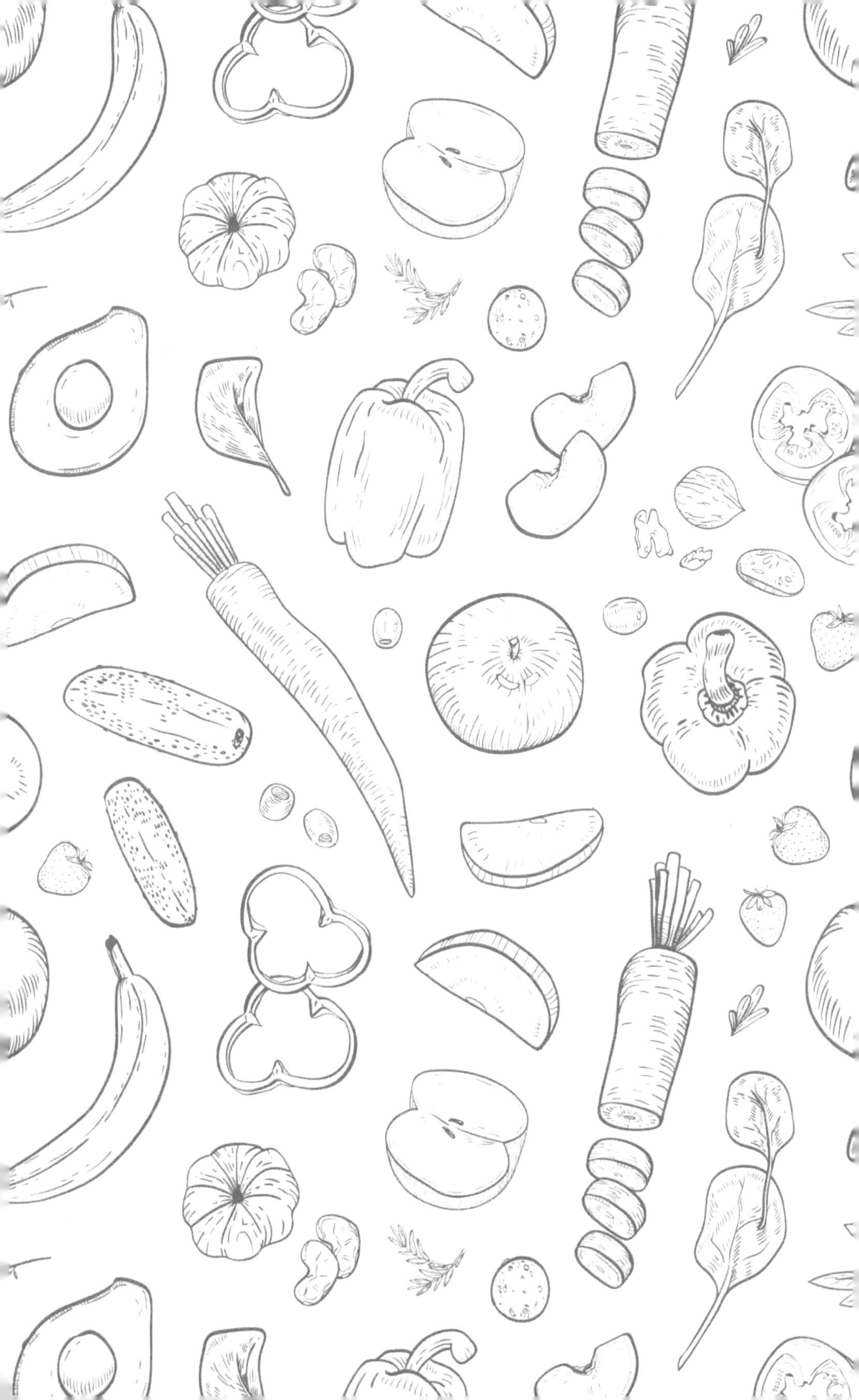

Krish Gupta

THE PICKLE GOES PUBLIC

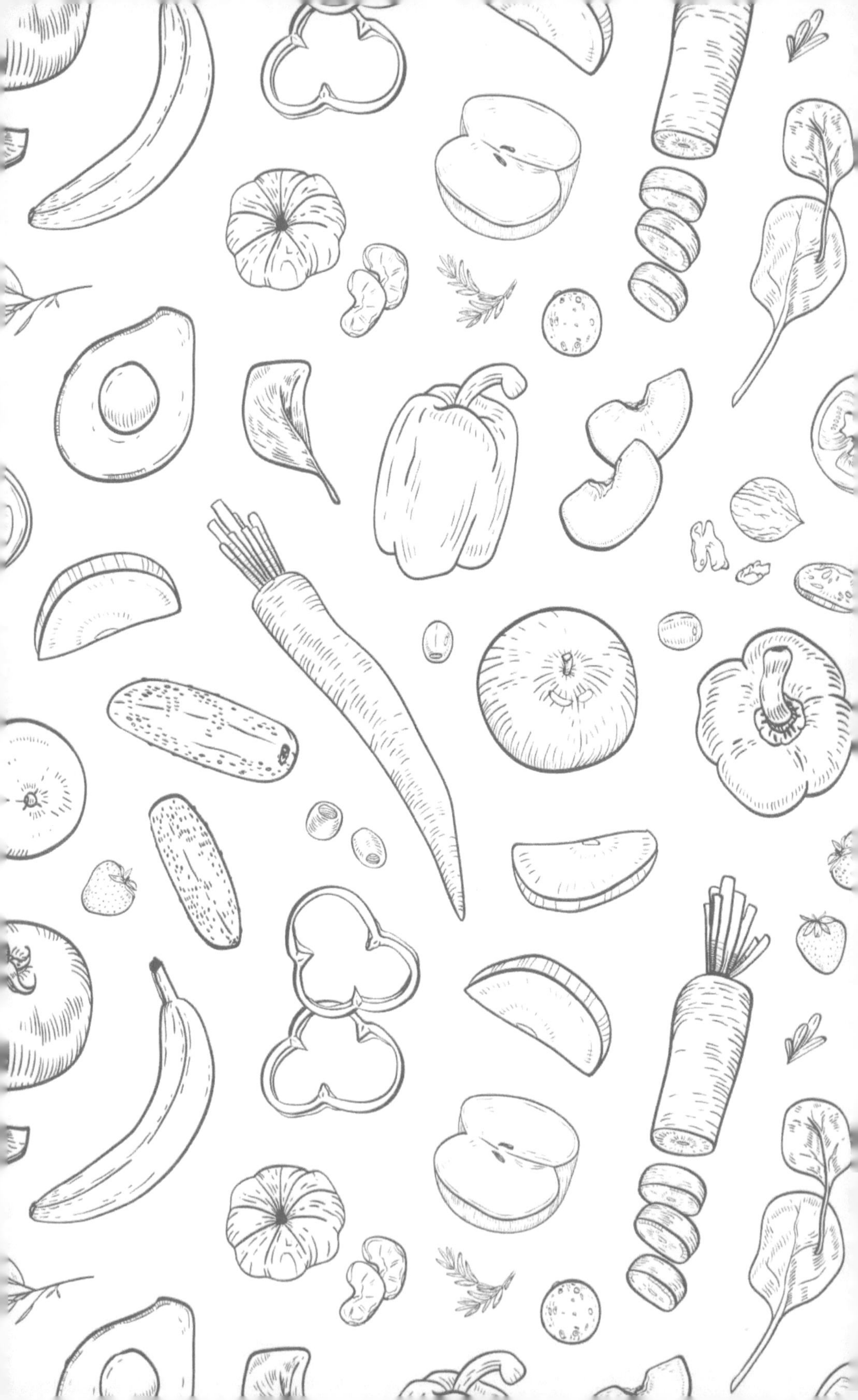

A month had elapsed since Rekha's trial batch of pickles with the sodium benzoate preservative had turned out perfectly, and the pickles were now ripe for retail. The duo were extremely excited about their venture, and it was all Piku could do to stop himself from digging into the jars that lined their kitchen counter.
However, both Rekha and Piku knew that they had to channel their excitement into an effective marketing strategy if they wanted their pickles to succeed in the market.
They put their heads together to brainstorm a distinctive selling proposition that would differentiate their pickles from the competition, keeping in mind key factors such as taste, texture, packaging, quantity, and pricing.
PIKU'S PICKLES

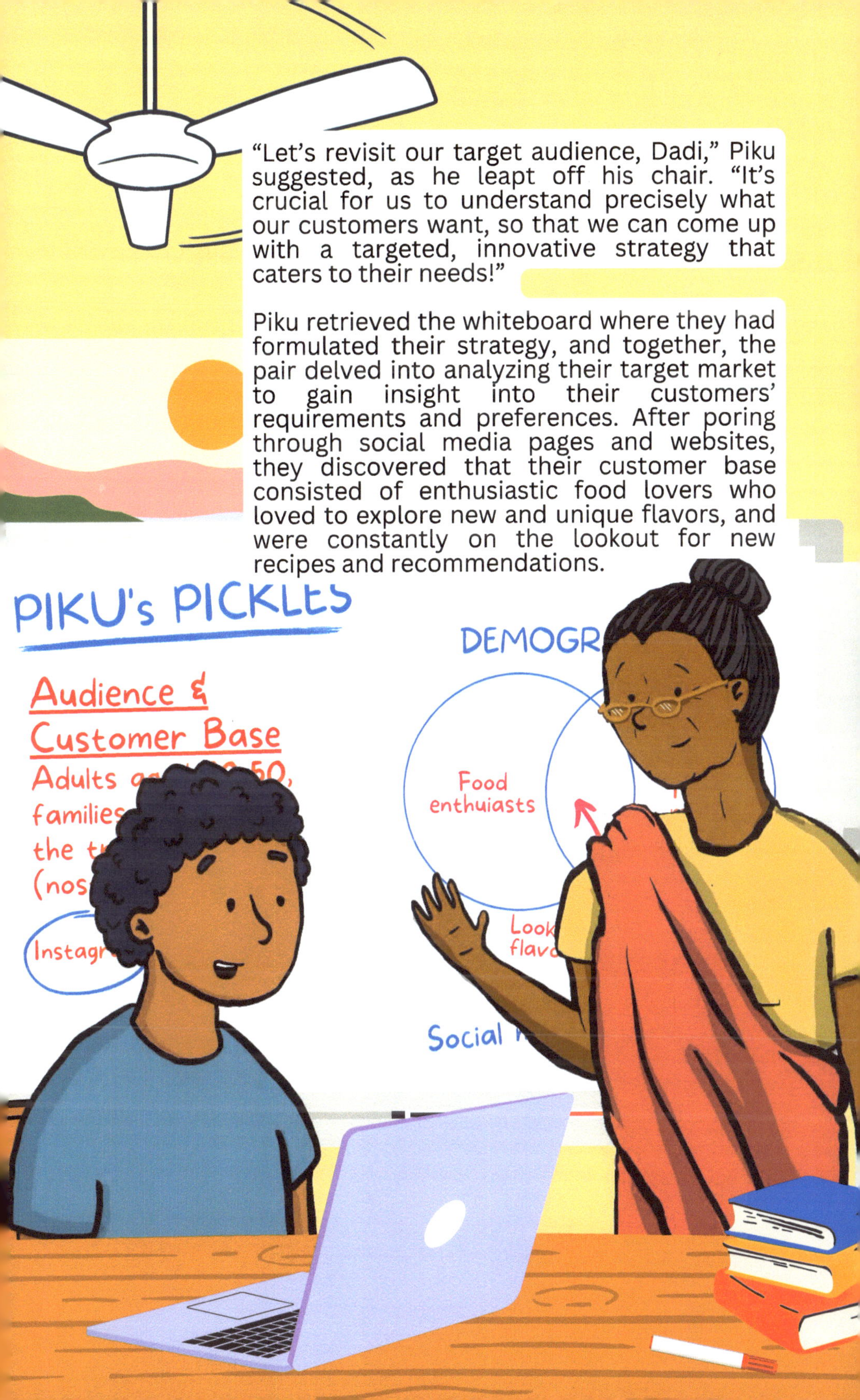

"Let's revisit our target audience, Dadi," Piku suggested, as he leapt off his chair. "It's crucial for us to understand precisely what our customers want, so that we can come up with a targeted, innovative strategy that caters to their needs!"

Piku retrieved the whiteboard where they had formulated their strategy, and together, the pair delved into analyzing their target market to gain insight into their customers' requirements and preferences. After poring through social media pages and websites, they discovered that their customer base consisted of enthusiastic food lovers who loved to explore new and unique flavors, and were constantly on the lookout for new recipes and recommendations.

“This information is fantastic!” exclaimed Piku with gusto. Rekha nodded in agreement, anticipating exactly where her grandson was headed with his idea. “We’ve already developed three distinct flavors and I’m confident they’ll have a unique taste unlike anything currently available in the market because they’re based on my mother’s special recipe,” Rekha said.

“Exactly!” Piku chimed in. “Now, all we need to do is include a different recipe suggestion for each flavor, and that will be our unique selling point!”

Rekha hugged Piku, suddenly feeling tremendously overwhelmed at her loving grandson’s unwavering support and enthusiasm. “Let’s get to work,” she said, with a warm smile.

Piku retrieved his treasured collection of felt-tip pens and vibrant chart paper that he often reserved for his best school projects, ready to begin an afternoon of careful preparation. Both he and Rekha spent the next few hours meticulously crafting recipe cards, ensuring that the instructions were straightforward and the ingredients were easily available.

Recalling recipes from memory, Rekha dictated them to Piku as he diligently transcribed them onto the chart paper, before neatly cutting and pasting them onto each jar, alongside their bright red and yellow logos.

"The jars look so good, Dadi!" Piku said, as he gestured towards the finished product. Indeed, the custom packaging was eye-catching, and the handwritten recipe cards added to the jars' distinctive appeal.

"Let me take a picture of you holding a jar, Piku!" Rekha said, and her grandson obliged, grinning proudly as he held up the colorful jar. "Wait, that's it!" he exclaimed, as Rekha appreciated the picture she had just taken. "We should take proper pictures of the jars and put them up on social media as part of our marketing strategy. This way, we'll be able to reach a wider audience and create some buzz around your pickles before actually selling them!"

Rekha observed intently as Piku created an Instagram account named 'Piku's Pickles' and began to upload pictures of the pickles along with their recipe suggestions. She also reluctantly posed for a picture with the pickle jars, upon Piku's insistence that followers would want to see the person responsible for making the delicious pickles.

Social media marketing was a completely new phenomenon for Rekha but she was eager to learn, and listened attentively as Piku explained that their follower count was already growing and their posts were quickly reaching a wider audience, which were promising signs for a brand new page.

A few weeks had passed since the launch of their Instagram page, and Piku ensured that they were engaging with their followers regularly, answering questions and responding to comments about the pickles. This helped to create a sense of community and made their followers feel like they were part of something special. Within just 15 days, they had amassed 3000 followers.

"Dadi, this is amazing!" Piku said, his eyes glimmering with excitement. "Your pickles are going to be a big hit!" Rekha smiled, sharing in Piku's zeal. "But when do we start selling the pickles Piku?" she asked, her voice giving away a hint of impatience.

“We’re almost there, Dadi,” Piku explained patiently. “We should aim to launch the pickles in two weeks. By then, we will have generated enough interest and our customers will be eager to sample your delicious pickles! Let’s brainstorm on a few other marketing tactics we can employ before the big day to ensure maximum impact.”

After putting their heads together, Piku and Rekha decided to create promotional videos on Instagram to showcase the versatility of the pickles.

They demonstrated how customers could pair their pickles with various foods, from parathas to rice and dal. They made sure to incorporate their recipe suggestions in the videos, so customers could see how effortlessly they could use the product. They also created a colorful poster announcing their much-awaited launch, offering delivery and pick-up services from Rekha’s house, as well as an early-bird discount of 10% off for customers who purchased all three flavors.

And with that, the dynamic duo sat back and watched as their marketing strategies took off, counting down the days to their first sale.

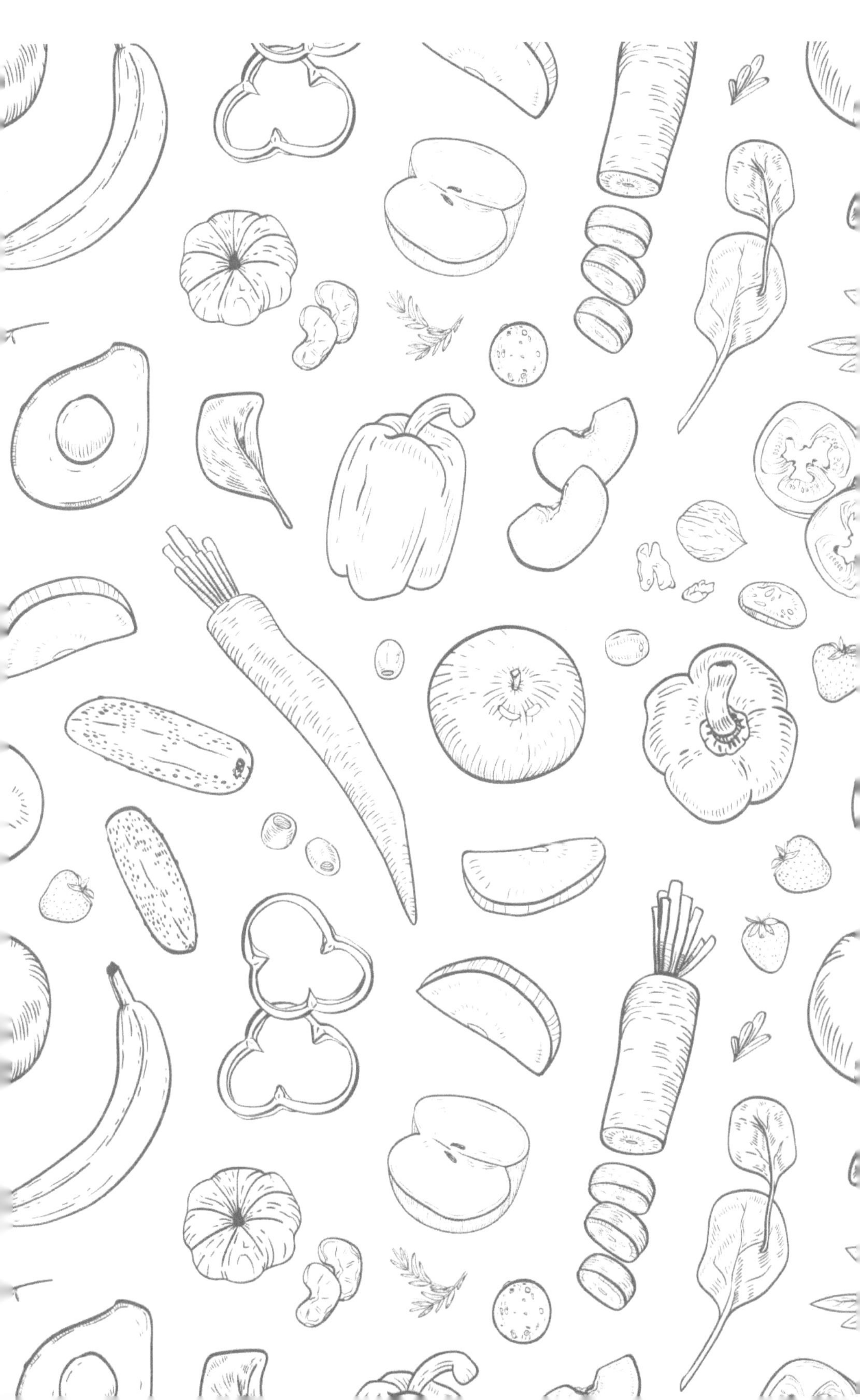

1
1
Krish Gupta

THE PICKLE
PROFITS
Krish Gupta

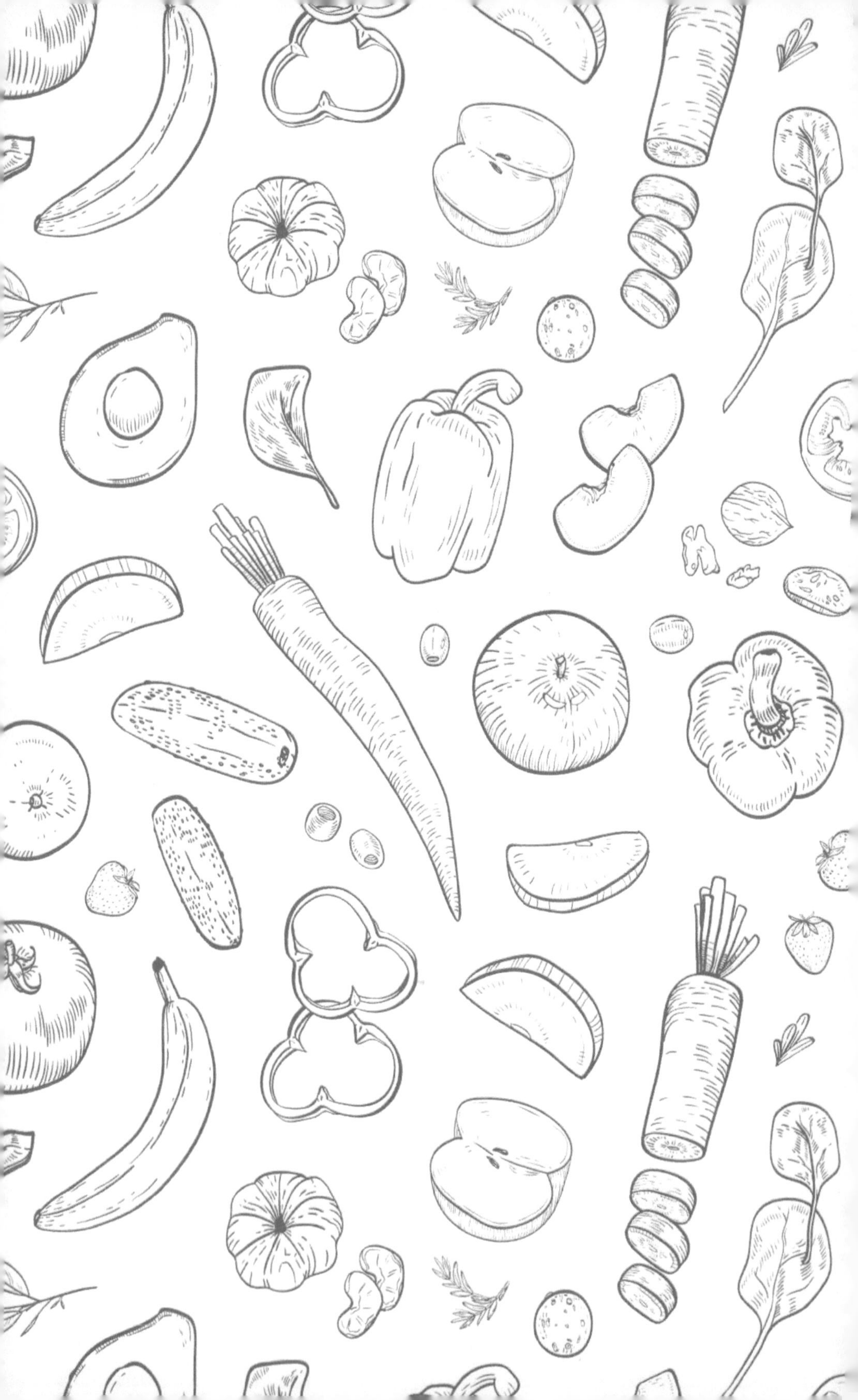

The highly anticipated day had finally arrived, and Piku and Rekha were brimming with excitement as they meticulously packed jars of their homemade pickles into boxes. Their social media following had generated an overwhelming number of orders, and they had decided to kickstart their venture with delivery and pick-up services from Rekha's home. Piku had even created a comprehensive delivery schedule to ensure prompt deliveries for their customers.
As he tied the last box, Piku confidently reassured his grandmother, "We're going to do great, Dadi." Rekha beamed at him with pride and responded, "I know we will. We've put in tireless effort to make this happen, and I couldn't be prouder of all that we've achieved so far."
PICKLE
PIKU'S
PICKLES

As the day progressed, Piku and Rekha received several messages from their customers, expressing how much they were looking forward to trying their pickles. Piku took the time to respond to each message personally, expressing gratitude for their constant support, and ensuring that their orders were on track.

When the first customer arrived to pick up their order, Rekha and Piku were overjoyed. They had dedicated so much time and effort to prepare for this day, and it was immensely gratifying that it was finally happening. They greeted the customer with warm smiles, handing over a jar of pickles along with a personalized note from Rekha, expressing her heartfelt thanks for their patronage.

As the day progressed, a steady stream of customers arrived to collect their orders. Piku and Rekha were kept busy, packing multiple jars of pickles and ensuring that everything was running smoothly.
At the end of the day, the duo sat down in the kitchen to tally their earnings. They were thrilled to discover that they had sold out all their jars and had made a decent profit. “We did it, Dadi!” Piku exclaimed, hugging his grandmother tightly. “We’ve successfully started our own business!” Rekha’s smile spoke volumes of her pride and sense of accomplishment. She had always known her pickles were special, but now the world knew it too.

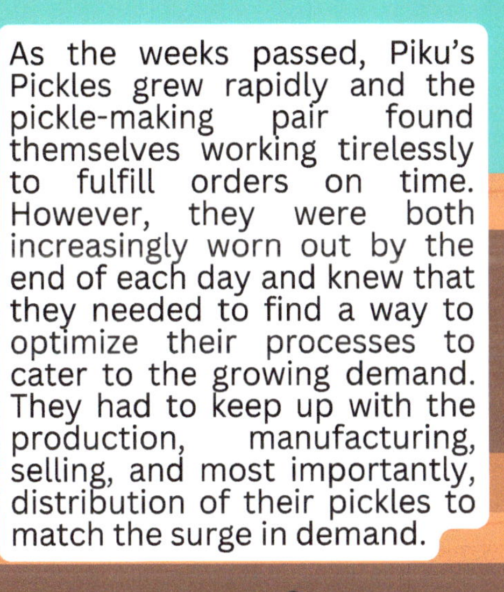

As the weeks passed, Piku's Pickles grew rapidly and the pickle-making pair found themselves working tirelessly to fulfill orders on time. However, they were both increasingly worn out by the end of each day and knew that they needed to find a way to optimize their processes to cater to the growing demand. They had to keep up with the production, manufacturing, selling, and most importantly, distribution of their pickles to match the surge in demand.

"We already have the best ingredients and recipe suggestions, but we need to find a more efficient way of making our pickles," Rekha observed. Piku nodded in agreement. "We should research and experiment with different methods of pickling to ensure that we're making the most of our time and resources," he suggested.

Piku opened his laptop to scour the internet for potential solutions, running each one by Rekha so she could use her expert judgment to determine its viability. They spent hours testing and tweaking their production process until they found the most efficient way to make their pickles. They honed their skills in sterilizing the jars, expertly mixing the ingredients, and properly storing the pickles to ensure optimal freshness.
“Piku, this looks fantastic,” Rekha exclaimed. “We’ve used the perfect combination of traditional methods and modern techniques, and those new-fangled preservatives you found online have increased our pickles’ shelf-life!” Piku nodded emphatically, beaming with pride. “Yes, Dadi! Now, it’s time for us to focus on ramping up our production process and manufacturing our pickles on a larger scale,” he said.

"I think we need a larger working space," Piku said to his grandmother, as he surveyed their cramped kitchen that was overflowing with pickle mixture and jars. "You're right," Rekha agreed. "Let's rent a commercial kitchen space and invest in large-scale equipment to accommodate the larger batches of pickles that we'll need to make to handle the demand for our pickles. We should be able to cover the costs with our profits so far, and we'll definitely benefit by working at a more efficient pace."

"We should also hire an assistant to help us with the manufacturing process!" Piku said. "Are you getting tired of helping your old Dadi, Piku?" Rekha teased. "Let's take it one step at a time. We need to make sure our costs don't outweigh the profits, right? If the need arises, we can definitely look into hiring one."

Piku and Rekha finally settled on a small commercial kitchen close to their home. Although it wasn't extravagant, it was significantly larger than Rekha's home kitchen and provided ample space to prepare and package the pickles. The duo had also bought large-scale equipment including industrial-sized vessels, ladles, and jars for making and storing their pickles. After setting up the new kitchen, they both stood back to admire their progress.
"Wow, Dadi, this is a huge step up!" Piku exclaimed with glee. "It looks so professional. We're becoming real business owners now, aren't we?" Rekha chuckled as she affectionately ruffled his hair. "Yes, but there's still lots to be done. Time to get to work, Piku," she reminded him, as they went about setting up proper quality control measures, making sure that every jar of pickle that left their facility would be up to their standards.
PIKU'S
PICKLES

Now that their production and manufacturing processes were in place, Rekha and Piku had to devise an efficient way to sell and distribute their pickles. Their initial home delivery and pick-up services had been extremely successful. However with their expanding customer base, they could no longer manage deliveries themselves, especially as some of their customers lived quite far away.

“Let's collaborate with local stores and cafes to sell our pickles. We can offer them a discount on bulk purchases and regularly replenish their stock. We should also create an online store where customers can purchase our pickles directly and partner with a local delivery service to handle the shipping and delivery,” Piku suggested. “That’s a brilliant idea, Piku,” Rekha enthused. “Sounds like a plan!”

As Piku and Rekha's business plan took off, they made sure to track their sales and demand regularly to ensure that they were meeting the needs of their customers. They also knew that they had to keep up with the changing needs of their customers so they started to offer new flavors and recipe suggestions to keep their product fresh and exciting.

"We should attend more events and farmers' markets to showcase our product and interact with customers," said Piku. Rekha agreed, "We'll take enough samples and promotional materials to each event to make a lasting impression."

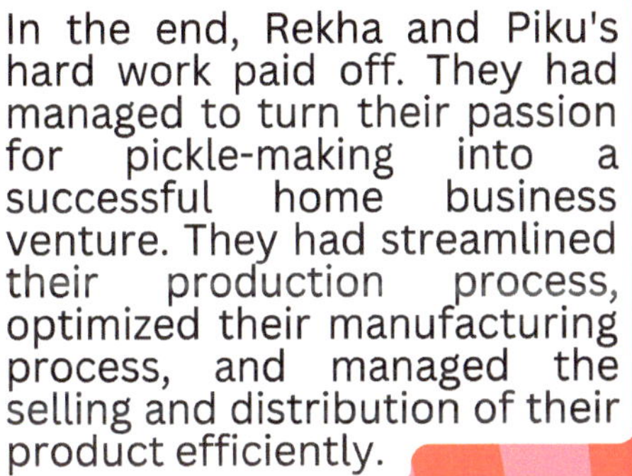

In the end, Rekha and Piku's hard work paid off. They had managed to turn their passion for pickle-making into a successful home business venture. They had streamlined their production process, optimized their manufacturing process, and managed the selling and distribution of their product efficiently.

"We've learned valuable lessons along the way," Rekha said to Piku. "We know that managing the operations of our business is key to our success, and there is no substitute for hard work. I also want to thank you from the bottom of my heart, Piku, for believing in me and making this dream come true. You're the best business partner and my biggest supporter!" she said, as she hugged her grandson with tears in her eyes.

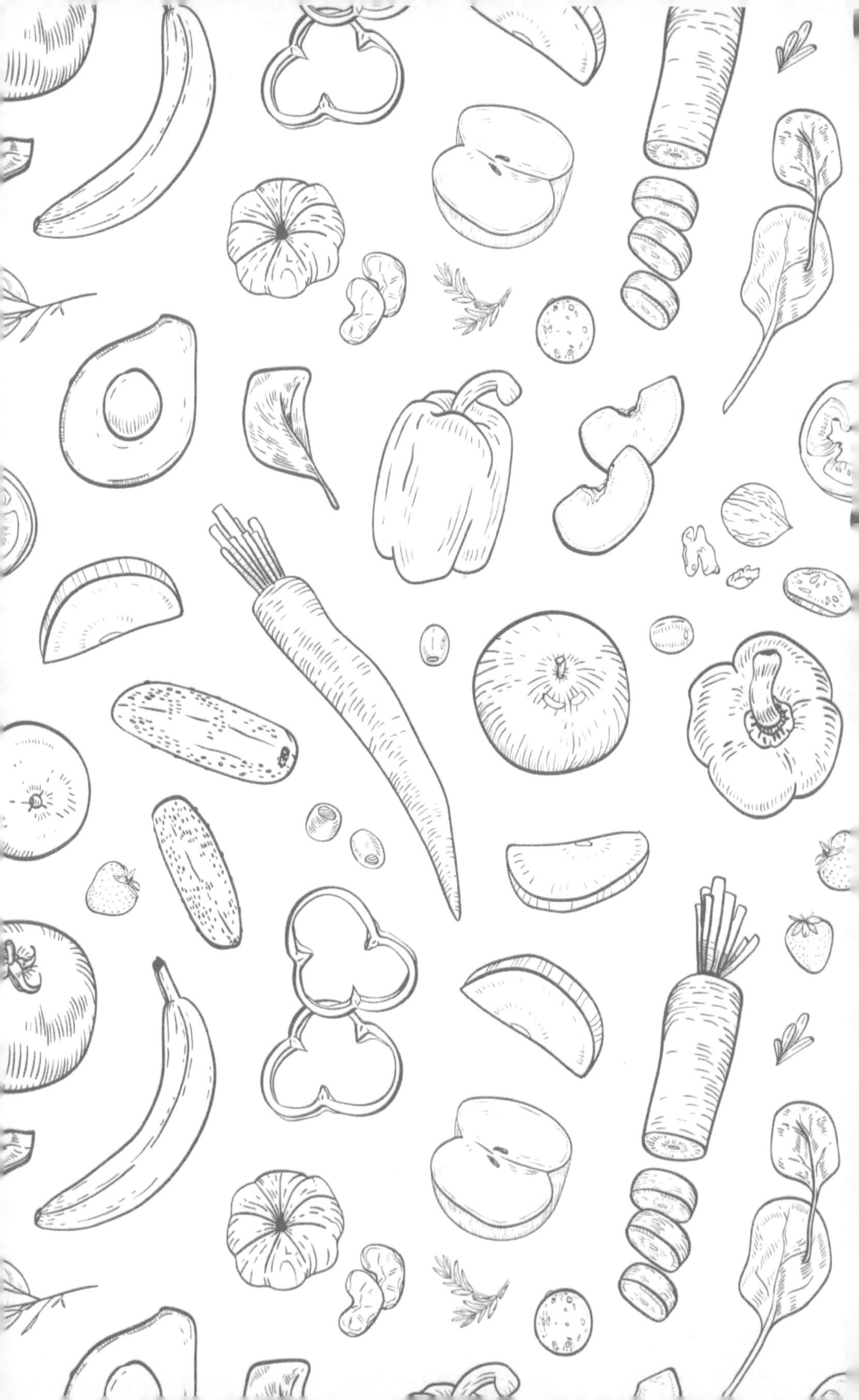

Krish Gupta

www.ingramcontent.com/pod-product-compliance
Lightning Source LLC
LaVergne TN
LVHW021344160826
845679LV00008B/1479

9798890267269